MOCKTAILS

EASY LOW-SUGAR NON-ALCOHOLIC RECIPES

Mocktails

Introduction

Welcome to the vibrant world of mocktails!

We invite you to embark on an exciting culinary adventure to discover all the possibilities mocktails offer. Whether seeking a healthier alternative, abstaining from alcohol, or looking for new flavor combinations, this book is your go-to guide.

With a growing emphasis on wellness and conscious drinking, people are seeking alternatives that offer all the sophistication and enjoyment of traditional cocktails without the alcoholic content. Mocktails, or "mock cocktails", have evolved from simple virgin versions of popular drinks to innovative and creative concoctions that dazzle the taste buds with unique flavors and stunning presentations.

We have selected over 80 recipes covering a range of ingredients, from fruits to aromatic herbs and botanicals. We encourage you to embrace your creativity and experiment with the recipes. Mix and match ingredients, adjust sweetness levels, and garnish with flair to create your signature mocktail masterpieces. The possibilities are endless!

Beyond the recipes, we will explore different glassware options, garnish styles, and presentation ideas, allowing you to showcase your mocktails with the elegance they deserve. We also celebrate the joy of sharing mocktails with friends and loved ones. We offer suggestions for pairing mocktails with delectable bites and creating a vibrant and inviting ambiance that enhances the overall enjoyment of the mocktails.

So we invite you to raise your glass and explore the captivating world of non-alcoholic libations.

Cheers to the endless possibilities of mocktails!

Basic Equipment

Used to strain out ice, fruit pulp, or other solid ingredients when pouring the mocktail into a glass

Designed to fit over a shaker tin and strain mixed drinks into a serving glass. Its distinguishing feature is the coiled spring around the disc, which helps hold it in place while allowing liquid to flow through

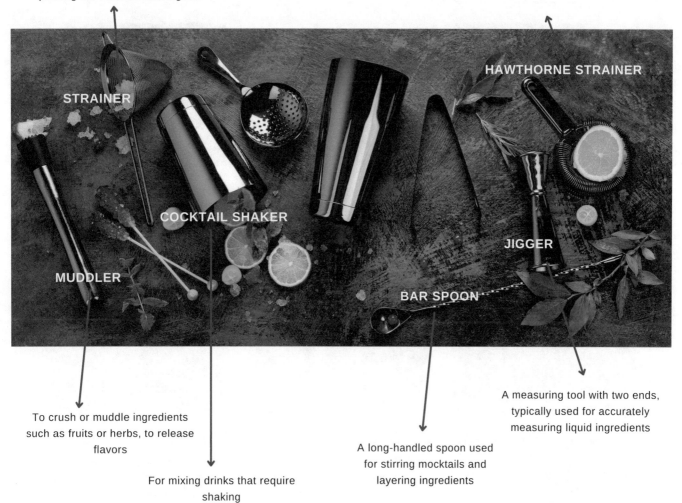

STRAINER

HAWTHORNE STRAINER

COCKTAIL SHAKER

JIGGER

MUDDLER

BAR SPOON

To crush or muddle ingredients such as fruits or herbs, to release flavors

For mixing drinks that require shaking

A long-handled spoon used for stirring mocktails and layering ingredients

A measuring tool with two ends, typically used for accurately measuring liquid ingredients

Mocktail Glasses

The visual presentation of mocktails is as important as the taste itself. The right glassware, thoughtful garnishes, and creative presentation can elevate a mocktail from a simple drink to a captivating sensory experience. Feel free to experiment and use different glassware to create your own unique mocktail presentations and enhance the overall drinking experience.

It is perfect for showcasing mocktails with plenty of ice and carbonated mixers like mojitos or fruit-based mocktails.

Designed for mocktails served over ice cubes and with a strong flavor profile, like mocktail versions of classic cocktails such as the margarita.

It works well for elegant mocktails with subtle flavors and delicate textures such as fizzes, and elegant herbal or citrus-based drinks.

It is great for mocktails showcasing vibrant colors, delicate flavors, and a touch of effervescence, such as fruity aperitifs.

Mocktails that incorporate sparkling water are well-suited for this glass. Its slender shape showcases the bubbles and allows for the appreciation of the drink's aromas.

Rustic and charming, it works well for informal and playful mocktails, such as fruity blends or lemonades, evoking a sense of nostalgia and relaxation.

Garnishes

Garnishes improve the mocktails' overall flavor profile and visual attractiveness. Let your imagination soar as you craft mocktails that are as visually captivating as delicious.

Citrus Twists or Wheels

They add a burst of vibrant color and a refreshing aroma. They work well with many drinks, from tangy margaritas to zesty spritzers.

Fresh Herbs

Sprigs of fresh herbs like mint, basil, or rosemary add an elegant touch to mocktails and infuse them with enticing aromas. They can be used as a simple garnish or muddled into the drink for extra flavor.

Edible Flowers

Delicate and visually stunning, you can use edible flowers like lavender or hibiscus to add a touch of elegance as a floating garnish, or placed delicately on the rim of the glass.

Skewers laden with bite-sized fruit pieces or olives can add a playful element to mocktails. They are popular in mocktail versions of classic cocktails like the virgin martini or fruit-infused mocktails.

Frozen or Sugared Glass Rims

Dip the rim of your glass into water or flavored syrup, and then dip it into sugar or salt for an eye-catching frosted or sugared effect. This simple technique adds an extra touch of elegance and flavor.

Unique Ice Cubes

Elevate your mocktail presentation with creative ice cubes. Use silicone molds to freeze fruit juice, edible flowers, or herbs into ice cubes that complement the flavors of your mocktail. They add visual appeal and infuse subtle flavors as they melt.

Delectable Bites

Organizing a mocktail party is an excellent way to gather friends and loved ones for an evening of delicious drinks. To create a memorable experience, it's essential to pair your mocktails with delectable bites that complement and enhance the flavors of the beverages.

Choose appetizers that are easy to handle and guests can enjoy in one or two bites. Miniature versions of classic dishes, such as sliders, bruschetta, or stuffed mushrooms, work well for a mocktail party. Additionally, consider serving small bowls of nuts, olives, or vegetable crudité with flavorful dips to provide a refreshing palate cleanser between sips.

Look for flavors that harmonize with the mocktails. If you have a citrus-based mocktail, consider appetizers with hints of citrus, like lemon-infused shrimp skewers. For mocktails with herbal undertones, try serving herbed goat cheese crostini or caprese skewers with fresh basil.

Create a pleasing contrast of textures by offering a combination of crispy, creamy, and crunchy appetizers. For example, pair a refreshing cucumber mocktail with crunchy vegetable spring rolls or serve a creamy spinach and artichoke dip alongside a sparkling berry mocktail.

Coordinate the garnishes of your mocktails with the flavors and ingredients of the paired appetizers. Use similar herbs and fruits in mocktails and appetizers to create a cohesive and visually appealing experience. For example, garnish a watermelon mocktail with a small watermelon cube skewered with feta cheese for a refreshing and elegant touch.

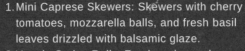

1. Mini Caprese Skewers: Skewers with cherry tomatoes, mozzarella balls, and fresh basil leaves drizzled with balsamic glaze.
2. Veggie Spring Rolls: Fresh and crunchy spring rolls filled with vegetables and served with a dipping sauce.
3. Bruschetta: Toasted baguette slices topped with diced tomatoes, fresh basil, garlic, and a drizzle of olive oil.
4. Spinach and Feta Stuffed Mushrooms: Button mushrooms filled with a mixture of spinach, feta cheese, and breadcrumbs.
5. Mini Quiches: Bite-sized quiches filled with various ingredients like cheese, vegetables, or ham.
6. Cucumber Bites: Cucumber slices topped with cream cheese, smoked salmon, or diced avocado.
7. Vegetable Crudité: Assorted raw vegetables like carrot sticks, celery, bell peppers, and cherry tomatoes served with a flavorful dip.
8. Mini Pita Pizzas: Mini pita bread topped with tomato sauce, cheese, and your favorite pizza toppings.
9. Sweet Potato Fries: Baked or fried sweet potato fries served with a dipping sauce.
10. Coconut Shrimp: Crunchy shrimp coated in coconut flakes and served with a tangy dipping sauce.
11. Cheese and Crackers: Assorted cheeses paired with a variety of crackers and fresh fruit slices.
12. Stuffed Dates: Dates filled with cream cheese, goat cheese, or almond butter, and optionally wrapped in bacon.
13. Mini Chicken Skewers: Bite-sized chicken skewers marinated in flavorful spices and grilled to perfection.
14. Sushi Rolls: Assorted sushi rolls with vegetarian or seafood fillings, served with soy sauce and wasabi.
15. Spicy Chicken Wings: Chicken wings coated in a spicy glaze and baked or fried until crispy.

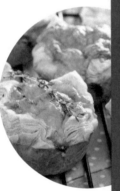

Tips & Tricks

1   Soda water can be substituted for another type of sparkling water, unflavored or with lemon or lime flavor.

2   Fruits and vegetables must be fresh because they create a brighter flavor than most pre-made mixes or artificial syrups. If you use fruit juices, try buying organic.

3   Crushed ice can be substituted for whole ice cubes, or omitted. If you don't have an ice crusher, crush ice cubes by placing them in a sealed plastic bag inside a clean kitchen towel, and then use a wooden spoon as a hammer to crush the ice.

4   Shaking ice in a cocktail shaker will chill the drink and create a frothy texture while stirring gently in a mixing glass maintains a smoother, lighter consistency.

5   For recipes using mint, use the leaves only, as the stem can make it bitter. If you don't have a muddler, use the handle of a wooden spoon instead. Don't muddle too much as the mint leaves can turn bitter.

Measurement Conversion Chart

Volume

U.S	IMPERIAL	METRIC
1 tablespoon	1/2 fl oz	15 ml
2 tablespoons	1 fl oz	30 ml
1/4 cup	2 fl oz	60 ml
1/3 cup	3 fl oz	90 ml
1/2 cup	4 fl oz	120 ml
2/3 cup	5 fl oz	150 ml
3/4 cup	6 fl oz	180 ml
1 cup	8 fl oz	240 ml
1 1/4 cup	10 fl oz	300 ml
2 cups	16 fl oz	480 ml
2 1/2 cups	20 fl oz	600 ml
1 quart	32 fl oz	1 l

Length

INCH	METRIC
1/4 inch	6 mm
1/2 inch	1,25 cm
3/3 inch	2 cm
1 inch	2,5 cm
6 inches	15 cm
12 inches	30 cm

Weight

U.S./IMPERIAL	METRIC
1/2 oz	15 g
1 oz	30 g
2 oz	60 g
1/4 lb	115 g
1/3 lb	150 g
1/2 lb	225 g
3/4 lb	350 g
1 lb	450 g

MOCKTAIL MAGIC RECIPES

- 1 cup (240 ml) apple juice
- 1 cinnamon stick
- 1 tablespoon fresh lemon juice
- 1 cup (240 ml) sparkling water
- Ice cubes
- Apple slice and ground cinnamon for garnish (optional)

STEPS

1. In a small saucepan, heat the apple juice with the cinnamon stick over low heat for 5 minutes.
2. Remove from heat and let it cool.
3. In a glass, combine the cooled apple juice, fresh lemon juice, and sparkling water. Stir well.
4. Fill the glass with ice cubes and garnish with an apple slice or a sprinkle of ground cinnamon, if desired.

NUTRITIONAL FACTS & SERVING SUGGESTIONS

Apples are a good source of vitamin C and dietary fiber, which help support immune function and digestive health.

Baked Brie with Apple Slices: Preheat the oven to 350°F (175°C). Take a round of Brie cheese and place it on a baking sheet. Bake until the cheese is slightly melted. Meanwhile, slice 1-2 apples into thin wedges. Once the Brie is done, transfer it to a serving platter and arrange the apple slices around it. Optional: drizzle the baked Brie with a touch of honey or sprinkle with chopped walnuts.

APPLE FIZZ MOCKTAIL

- 1 cup (240 ml) apple juice
- 1/2 cup (120 ml) sparkling water
- 1 tablespoon lemon juice
- Ice cubes
- Apple slices for garnish (optional)

STEPS

1. Fill a glass with ice cubes.
2. Pour the apple juice into the glass.
3. Add the sparkling water and lemon juice.
4. Stir gently to mix the ingredients.
5. Garnish with a slice of apple.
6. Serve chilled and enjoy!

NUTRITIONAL FACTS & SERVING SUGGESTIONS

Apple and Goat Cheese Crostini: Preheat the oven to 350°F (175°C). Take a baguette and slice it into thin rounds. Arrange the slices on a baking sheet and lightly toast them in the oven for a few minutes until they become crispy. Meanwhile, slice a small wedge of goat cheese and thinly slice an apple. Once the crostini slices are toasted, spread a layer of goat cheese on each slice and top it with a couple of apple slices. Place the crostini back in the oven for a few more minutes until the cheese melts slightly.

BANANA COLADA

- 1 ripe banana
- 1/2 cup (120 ml) pineapple juice
- 1/2 cup (120 ml) coconut milk
- 1/2 cup crushed ice (around 6 ices cubes)
- Pineapple wedge for garnish (optional)

NUTRITIONAL FACTS & SERVING SUGGESTIONS

Bananas are rich in potassium, vitamin B6, and dietary fiber, making them a great choice for maintaining heart health and promoting digestion.

Coconut Shrimp: 12 large peeled and deveined shrimp. In a bowl, combine 1/2 cup flour, 1/2 teaspoon salt, 1/4 teaspoon black pepper, 1/4 teaspoon paprika, and 1/4 teaspoon garlic powder. Coat the shrimp with this flour mixture, then dip them in beaten egg and coat with shredded coconut and breadcrumbs. Refrigerate for 15-20 minutes. Fry in hot vegetable oil until golden and crispy. Serve hot as an appetizer, optionally with sweet chili sauce.

STEPS

1. In a blender, combine the ripe banana, pineapple juice, coconut milk, and crushed ice.
2. Blend until smooth and creamy.
3. Pour the mixture into a glass.
4. Garnish with a pineapple wedge and cherry.

INGREDIENTS (1 SERVING)

- 1 medium-sized beetroot, cooked and peeled
- 1 orange, juiced
- 1/2 lemon, juiced
- 1 tablespoon honey (adjust to taste)
- Soda water or sparkling water
- Ice cubes
- Orange slice or mint sprig, for garnish

NUTRITIONAL FACTS & SERVING SUGGESTIONS

Beets are rich in folate, manganese, and dietary fiber. They also provide a good amount of vitamin C and potassium.

Mediterranean Hummus Dip with Veggie Sticks: Transfer the hummus to a serving bowl, spreading it evenly. Arrange the vegetable sticks around the hummus bowl for dipping. Drizzle a little olive oil over the hummus for added richness.

STEPS

1. In a blender, add the cooked and peeled beetroot, freshly squeezed orange juice, lemon juice, and honey.
2. Blend until smooth and well combined.
3. Fill a glass with ice cubes.
4. Pour the beetroot mixture over the ice, filling the glass about halfway.
5. Top up the glass with soda water or sparkling water.
6. Stir gently to combine the flavors.
7. Garnish with an orange slice or mint sprig, if desired.

- 1/2 cup (120 ml) fruit puree (such as peach or strawberry)
- 3/4 cup (180 ml) sparkling water or non-alcoholic sparkling wine
- Fresh fruit slices or mint leaves for garnish (optional)

STEPS

1. In a blender, blend the fruit puree until smooth.
2. Pour the fruit puree into a flute glass.
3. Slowly pour the sparkling water or non-alcoholic sparkling wine over the fruit puree.
4. Stir gently to combine.
5. Garnish with fresh fruit slices or mint leaves, if desired.

NUTRITIONAL FACTS & SERVING SUGGESTIONS

Peaches provide a good source of vitamins A and C, as well as dietary fiber, making them beneficial for immune support, skin health, and promoting healthy digestion.

Bruschetta: Slice a baguette into thin slices and toast them until crispy. In a bowl, combine 2 diced tomatoes, 2 cloves of minced garlic, fresh basil, 2 tbsp olive oil, 1 tbsp balsamic vinegar, salt, and pepper. Spoon the tomato mixture onto the toasted baguette slices.

BERRY BLAST

INGREDIENTS (1-2 SERVINGS)

- 1 cup (240 ml) mixed berries (such as strawberries, raspberries, or blueberries)
- 1/2 (120 ml) cup water
- 1 tablespoon fresh lemon juice
- 1-2 teaspoons low-sugar sweetener (e.g., stevia, agave syrup, honey)
- 1 cup (240 ml) sparkling water
- Ice cubes
- Fresh berries and mint leaves for garnish (optional)

STEPS

1. In a blender, combine the berries, water, lemon juice, and sweetener. Blend until smooth.
2. Strain the mixture through a fine mesh sieve (optional if you prefer a smoother texture).
3. Fill glasses with ice cubes. Pour the berry mixture, filling them about halfway.
4. Top with sparkling water.
5. Garnish with fresh berries and mint leaves and serve chilled.

NUTRITIONAL FACTS & SERVING SUGGESTIONS

Berry and Spinach Salad Cups: Take small serving cups or bowls. Fill each cup with a handful of fresh spinach leaves. Top the spinach with a mix of mixed berries. Sprinkle crumbled feta cheese over the berries. Add a sprinkle of chopped walnuts or almonds for crunch. Drizzle balsamic glaze or vinaigrette dressing over the salad.

BLACKBERRY GINGER FIZZ

INGREDIENTS (1 SERVING)

- 2/3 cup (150 ml) ginger ale or sparkling water
- 2 tablespoons (30 ml) blackberry syrup
- Blackberries and a mint sprig for garnish (optional)

STEPS

1. Add the ginger ale and blackberry syrup to a glass with ice.
2. Give the mixture a gentle stir.
3. Garnish with skewered blackberries and a mint sprig and serve.

NUTRITIONAL FACTS & SERVING SUGGESTIONS

Blackberries are a nutritious fruit packed with vitamins C and K, dietary fiber, and antioxidants.

Goat Cheese and Walnut-Stuffed Mushrooms: Preheat oven to 375°F (190°C). Clean 4 large button mushrooms. In a bowl, combine 2 ounces of goat cheese, 2 tablespoons of chopped walnuts, minced garlic, salt, and pepper. Stuff each mushroom with the mixture. Drizzle the mushrooms with 1 tablespoon of olive oil and season with salt and pepper. Bake until tender and golden brown.

INGREDIENTS (1 SERVING)

- 1/4 cup (60 ml) of black olive brine
- 1/4 cup (60 ml) of beet juice
- 2 tablespoons (30 ml) fresh lemon juice
- 1 ice cube
- Toothpick & 3 black olives (optional, to serve)

NUTRITIONAL FACTS & SERVING SUGGESTIONS

Bacon-Wrapped Jalapeño Poppers: Preheat oven to 400°F (200°C) and line a baking sheet with parchment paper. Slice and deseed 4 large jalapeño peppers. In a bowl, mix together 4 ounces of cream cheese and 1/4 cup of shredded cheddar cheese. Fill each jalapeño half with the cheese mixture. Wrap each jalapeño half with a halved slice of bacon and secure with a toothpick. Place the poppers on the baking sheet and bake for 15-20 minutes until crispy and peppers are tender. Allow to cool slightly before serving.

STEPS

1. Pour black olive brine, beet juice, and lemon juice, into a cocktail shaker and add an ice cube. Close the lid and shake well.
2. Pour in a martini glass and decorate with a toothpick with 3 black olives (optional).

BLOODY MARY MOCKTAIL

INGREDIENTS (2 SERVINGS)

- 2 ½ cups (600 ml) of tomato juice
- 4 tablespoons (60 ml) of green olive brine
- 1 garlic clove
- 1-2 teaspoons of hot sauce
- ½ of a cucumber peeled and chopped
- 1 celery rib, chopped
- Juice of ½ of a lemon
- 1 teaspoon of horseradish
- 1 teaspoon of Worcestershire sauce
- Ice
- Green olives and celery for garnish (optional)

STEPS

1. In a blender or food processor, add the tomato juice, olive brine, cucumber, celery, lemon juice, garlic clove, horseradish, hot sauce, and Worcestershire sauce and blend until smooth.
2. Pour over a glass of ice and garnish with celery and green olives.

NUTRITIONAL FACTS & SERVING SUGGESTIONS

Vegetable Crudités: Cut 1 carrot, 1 celery stalk, 1/2 bell pepper, cherry tomatoes 1/2 cucumber, 1/2 cup broccoli florets into bite-sized pieces. In a small bowl, mix together 1/2 cup of Greek yogurt, 1 tablespoon of lemon juice, 1/2 teaspoon of cumin, and season with salt and pepper. Place yogurt dip in the center of the platter.

INGREDIENTS (2 SERVINGS)

- 1 cup (150 g) fresh/frozen blueberries
- 4-5 fresh basil leaves
- Juice of 2 lemons
- 1 cup (240ml) sparkling water
- Ice cubes

NUTRITIONAL FACTS & SERVING SUGGESTIONS

Blueberries are packed with antioxidants, vitamin C, and vitamin K, contributing to brain health and cardiovascular support.

Watermelon and Feta Salad: Combine 2 cups of cubed watermelon and 100 g of crumbled feta cheese. Sprinkle 1/4 cup of chopped fresh mint leaves over the watermelon and feta. Drizzle 2 tablespoons of extra-virgin olive oil and 1 tablespoon of balsamic vinegar over the salad. Season with salt and black pepper to taste.

STEPS

1. In a blender, blend the fresh blueberries and basil leaves until smooth.
2. Strain the mixture through a fine-mesh sieve.
3. In a pitcher, combine the strained blueberry and basil mixture with the juice of 2 lemons and stir well.
4. Add sparkling water to the pitcher.
5. Fill glasses with ice cubes and pour the blueberry basil lemonade over the ice.
6. Garnish with fresh blueberries and a sprig of basil or mint (optional)

- 1/2 cup (120 ml) blueberries (fresh or frozen)
- 1/2 cup (120 ml) unsweetened coconut water
- 1/4 cup (60 ml) freshly squeezed lime juice
- 1-2 teaspoons low-sugar sweetener (e.g., stevia, agave syrup, honey)
- 1 cup (240 ml) sparkling water
- Ice cubes
- Blueberries skewer for garnish (optional)

Caprese Skewers: Take 12 skewers and thread one cherry tomato, followed by one small fresh mozzarella ball, and then one fresh basil leaf. Repeat this pattern until you have used all the ingredients. Drizzle balsamic glaze over the skewers, ensuring each skewer gets a touch of the glaze. Season with salt and black pepper to taste.

1. In a blender, combine the blueberries, coconut water, lime juice, and sweetener. Blend until smooth.
2. Fill serving glasses with ice cubes.
3. Pour the blueberry mixture into the glasses, filling them about halfway.
4. Top each glass with sparkling water or soda water to add a refreshing fizz.
5. Garnish with a blueberry skewer, a mint leaf or some lime (optional)
6. Serve chilled.

INGREDIENTS (1 SERVING)

- ½ lemon or lime
- 2 drops of blue food coloring optional
- ⅔ cups (150 ml) lemonade
- Ice
- 1 lemon slice (optional)

NUTRITIONAL FACTS & SERVING SUGGESTIONS

Cucumber Bites with Cream Cheese: Slice cucumbers into rounds and spread a layer of cream cheese on top. Optionally, garnish with a small dill sprig or a sprinkle of paprika. These refreshing and light bites provide a cool contrast to the zesty flavors of the mocktail.

STEPS

1. Peel the rind of the lemon or lime with a potato peeler, and squeeze out the juice.
2. Place the rind and lemon/lime juice in a glass and mash together using a muddler.
3. Add in the blue food coloring and mix.
4. Add in ice cubes and fill up with lemonade.
5. Garnish with a slice of lemon and serve.

CANTALOUPE AND GINGER RESFRESHER

- 1 cup (240 ml) melon juice (such as cantaloupe or honeydew)
- 1/4 cup (60 ml) ginger ale
- 1/4 cup (60 ml) sparkling water
- 1 tablespoon (15 ml) lime juice
- 1 teaspoon (5 ml) honey or agave syrup
- Ice cubes
- Melon balls and lime slices for garnish (optional)

STEPS

1. In a glass, combine the melon juice, ginger ale, sparkling water, lime juice, and honey (or agave syrup). Stir well to mix.
2. Fill the glass with ice cubes.
3. Garnish with melon balls and lime slices, if desired.

NUTRITIONAL FACTS & SERVING SUGGESTIONS

Melons are hydrating fruits that provide vitamin C, vitamin A, and electrolytes, promoting skin health and hydration.

Watermelon Halloumi Skewers: Skewer small cubes of fresh watermelon and chunks of Halloumi cheese on toothpicks or small skewers.

CARAMEL APPLE MOCKTAIL

- 1/4 cup (60 ml) apple cider
- 2 tablespoons (30 ml) caramel syrup
- 2 tablespoons (30 ml) lemon juice
- 1/4 cup (60 ml) sparkling water
- Apple slice and cinnamon stick, for garnish (optional)

NUTRITIONAL FACTS & SERVING SUGGESTIONS

Mini Puff Pastry Apple Turnovers: Preheat the oven to 400°F (200°C). Cut 1 sheet of puff pastry into 2 squares. In a bowl, combine 1 diced apple, 1 tbsp sugar, 1/2 tsp ground cinnamon, and 1/2 tsp lemon juice. Place half the mixture onto each puff pastry square, leaving a border around the edges. Fold diagonally to create a triangle shape, pressing the edges with a fork to seal. Brush the tops with a beaten egg. Bake until golden brown. Cool slightly before serving.

STEPS

1. In a glass, combine the apple cider, caramel syrup, and lemon juice.
2. Stir well to mix.
3. Add ice to the glass.
4. Top with sparkling water.
5. Garnish with an apple slice and a cinnamon stick.
6. Serve and enjoy!

CARAMEL DELIGHT

- 1 cup (240 ml) unsweetened almond milk (or any preferred milk alternative)
- 1/4 teaspoon caramel extract
- Ice cubes
- Caramel syrup (sugar-free) for drizzling (optional)

STEPS

1. In a glass, combine the unsweetened almond milk, and caramel extract. Stir well to dissolve the sweetener.
2. Fill the glass with ice cubes.
3. Drizzle sugar-free caramel syrup on top for extra flavor (optional).
4. Serve and enjoy!

NUTRITIONAL FACTS & SERVING SUGGESTIONS

Almond Butter Stuffed Dates: Using a small knife, make a lengthwise slit in 4 big dates and carefully remove the pit. Gently open up the dates to create a pocket for the almond butter. Spoon 1/2 tbsp of almond butter into each date, filling the cavity. If desired, sprinkle crushed almonds, and shredded coconut, or drizzle honey on top for added flavor and texture. Press the dates closed to seal the almond butter inside. Serve the almond butter stuffed dates as is, or chill them in the refrigerator for a firmer texture.

CHERRY COLADA

- 1 cup (240 ml) cherry juice
- 1/2 cup (120 ml) coconut milk
- 1/4 cup (60 ml) pineapple juice
- 1 tablespoon (15 ml) lime juice
- 1 cup (240 ml) crushed ice
- Maraschino cherries and pineapple wedges for garnish (optional)

STEPS

1. In a blender, combine the cherry juice, coconut milk, pineapple juice, lime juice, and crushed ice.
2. Blend until smooth and well combined.
3. Pour the mixture into a glass.
4. Garnish with maraschino cherries and pineapple wedges, if desired.
5. Serve the cherry colada mocktail immediately.

NUTRITIONAL FACTS & SERVING SUGGESTIONS

Cherries are rich in antioxidants and provide vitamin C, contributing to joint health, inflammation reduction, and immune support.

Fruit Skewers: Thread fresh cherries and pineapple chunks onto skewers for a vibrant and refreshing snack. The combination of juicy cherries and tropical pineapple complements the flavors of the mocktail, adding a burst of fruity goodness. For an optional twist, you can lightly grill the skewers to bring out the natural sweetness and enhance the flavors.

INGREDIENTS (1 SERVING)

- 1/2 cup (120 ml) cherry juice
- 1/4 cup (60 ml) fresh lime juice
- 8-10 fresh mint leaves
- 1 tablespoon (15 ml) honey or agave syrup
- 1 cup (240 ml) sparkling water
- Ice cubes
- Fresh cherries and mint sprigs for garnish (optional)

NUTRITIONAL FACTS & SERVING SUGGESTIONS

Smoked Salmon and Cucumber Bites: Slice 1 cucumber into thin rounds. Spread a small amount of cream cheese on each cucumber slice. Place a slice of smoked salmon on top of the cream cheese. Sprinkle fresh dill and a pinch of lemon zest over the salmon. Season with salt and pepper to taste.

STEPS

1. In a glass, muddle together the fresh mint leaves and honey (or agave syrup) to release the flavors.
2. Add the cherry juice and lime juice to the glass. Stir well to combine.
3. Fill the glass with ice cubes.
4. Top the mixture with sparkling water and gently stir.
5. Garnish with fresh cherries and mint sprigs, if desired.

INGREDIENTS (1 SERVING)

- 1/2 cup (120 ml) cold brew coffee
- 2 tablespoons (30 ml) pomegranate syrup
- 1/3 cup (90 ml) tonic water
- Orange peel twist to garnish (optional)

STEPS

1. In a glass, combine the cold brew coffee and pomegranate syrup. Stir well to mix.
2. Fill the glass with ice cubes.
3. Top the mixture with tonic water and gently stir.
4. Garnish with an orange peel twist.
5. Serve immediately and enjoy!

NUTRITIONAL FACTS & SERVING SUGGESTIONS

Dark Chocolate Energy Bites: Prepare small energy bites using a mixture of dates, nuts (such as almonds or walnuts), and unsweetened cocoa powder. These no-bake treats offer a rich and chocolatey flavor that complements the boldness of the coffee and the tanginess of the pomegranate syrup. They provide a satisfying and nutritious snack to enjoy alongside the mocktail.

- 1 orange, juiced
- 1 lemon, juiced
- 1 lime, juiced
- 1 cup sparkling water (240ml)
- Ice cubes

STEPS

1. In a pitcher, combine the freshly squeezed orange, lemon, and lime juice.
2. Add the sparkling water and stir gently to combine.
3. Fill two glasses with ice cubes and pour the citrus mixture over the ice.
4. Garnish with a slice of citrus fruit, if desired.
5. Serve and enjoy!

NUTRITIONAL FACTS & SERVING SUGGESTIONS

Citrus fruits, such as oranges, lemons, and limes, are rich in vitamin C, which acts as a powerful antioxidant, supporting the immune system and promoting the health of skin, bones, and blood vessels.

Mediterranean Hummus Cups: Fill small phyllo pastry cups with a generous spoonful of your favorite hummus. Top the hummus with a mixture of diced cucumbers, cherry tomatoes, and Kalamata olives. Sprinkle with crumbled feta cheese and a drizzle of olive oil.

INGREDIENTS (1 SERVING)

- 1/4 cup (60 ml) orange juice
- 1/4 cup (60 ml) cranberry juice
- 2 tablespoons (30 ml) lemon juice
- 2 tablespoons (30 ml) lime juice
- 1/4 cup (60 ml) sparkling water
- Mixed berries for garnish (optional)

STEPS

1. Fill a glass with ice.
2. Add the orange juice, cranberry juice, lemon juice, and lime juice to the glass.
3. Stir well to combine.
4. Top with sparkling water.
5. Garnish with mixed berries.
6. Serve and enjoy!

NUTRITIONAL FACTS & SERVING SUGGESTIONS

Cranberries are known for their antioxidants and provide vitamin C and dietary fiber, benefiting urinary tract health and immune function.

Herbed Cream Cheese Stuffed Mini Peppers: Slice the tops of 6 mini bell peppers and remove the seeds. In a mixing bowl, combine 4 oz cream cheese, 1 tbsp chopped fresh herbs, 1/2 tsp lemon juice, salt, and pepper. Mix well until thoroughly combined. Fill each mini pepper with the herbed cream cheese mixture, ensuring they are evenly filled.

COCONUT LIME COOLER

- 1 cup (240ml) coconut water
- Juice of 2 limes
- 1 tablespoon (15ml) agave syrup or honey
- 1 cup (240ml) sparkling water
- Ice cubes
- Slice of lime or sprig of mint to garnish (optional)

STEPS

1. In a glass, combine the coconut water, lime juice, and agave syrup.
2. Stir well to dissolve the sweetener.
3. Fill the glass with ice cubes and pour sparkling water over the ice.
4. Give it a gentle stir and garnish with a lime slice or a sprig of mint, if desired.

NUTRITIONAL FACTS & SERVING SUGGESTIONS

Thai Fresh Spring Rolls: Fill a large bowl with warm water. Dip one rice paper wrapper into the water for a few seconds until it becomes soft and pliable. Lay it flat on a clean surface. Arrange 2 cooked shrimp in the center of the rice paper wrapper. Layer a handful of mixed fresh vegetables on top of the shrimp. Sprinkle fresh herbs over the vegetables. Fold the sides of the rice paper wrapper towards the center, then tightly roll it up from the bottom, enclosing the filling. Repeat with the remaining rice paper wrappers. Serve with sweet chili sauce or peanut sauce.

- 1/4 cup (60 ml) pineapple juice
- 2 tablespoons (30 ml) coconut milk
- 2 tablespoons (30 ml) sparkling water
- 1 tablespoon (15 ml) lime juice
- Ice cubes
- Pineapple slice, for garnish (optional)

Pineapples contain vitamin C and manganese, as well as bromelain, an enzyme that aids digestion.

Fresh Fruit Salsa with Cinnamon Tortilla Chips: In a bowl, combine 1 cup mixed fresh fruits, 1 tbsp lime juice, 1 tbsp honey, and 1 tbsp chopped mint. Brush 4 tortillas with 1 tbsp melted butter. Mix 1 tbsp sugar and 1/2 tsp ground cinnamon in a separate bowl. Sprinkle the mixture evenly over both sides of the tortillas. Cut the tortillas into wedges and bake at 350°F (175°C) until crispy and lightly golden.

1. In a cocktail shaker, combine the pineapple juice, coconut milk, and lime juice.
2. Shake well to combine.
3. Strain the mixture into a glass filled with ice.
4. Top with sparkling water.
5. Garnish with a pineapple slice and serve.

- 1/4 cup (60 ml) cranberry juice
- 1/4 cup (60 ml) lime juice
- 1/4 cup (60 ml) orange juice
- 1-2 tablespoons honey
- Ice
- Orange peel, for garnish (optional)

STEPS

1. In a shaker, combine the cranberry juice, lime juice, orange juice, honey, and ice.
2. Shake until the ingredients are well mixed until the shaker is frosted.
3. Strain the mixture into a chilled martini glass.
4. Garnish with a twist of orange peel.

NUTRITIONAL FACTS & SERVING SUGGESTIONS

Baked Camembert Bites: Preheat the oven to 350°F (175°C). Place 6 mini phyllo pastry shells on a baking sheet. Add a small cube of Camembert cheese to each pastry shell. Drizzle about 1 teaspoon of honey over each cheese-filled pastry shell. Sprinkle a pinch of chopped nuts over each shell for added texture and flavor. Bake for approximately 10 minutes, or until the cheese has melted and the pastry shells are golden brown.

CRANBERRY GINGER SPARKLER

INGREDIENTS (1 SERVING)

- 1/2 cup (120 ml) cranberry juice
- 1/4 cup (60 ml) ginger ale
- 1/4 cup (60 ml) sparkling water
- 1 tablespoon (15 ml) lime juice
- 1 teaspoon (5 ml) honey or agave syrup
- Ice cubes
- Fresh cranberries and lime slices for garnish (optional)

STEPS

1. In a glass, combine the cranberry juice, ginger ale, sparkling water, lime juice, and honey (or agave syrup). Stir well to mix.
2. Fill the glass with ice cubes.
3. Garnish with fresh cranberries and lime slices, if desired.

NUTRITIONAL FACTS & SERVING SUGGESTIONS

Cranberries are known for their antioxidants and provide vitamin C and dietary fiber, benefiting urinary tract health and immune function.

Glazed Chicken Skewers: Marinate for at least 30 min 2 boneless, skinless chicken breasts, cut into bite-sized pieces in a mixture of 1 tbsp lime juice, 2 tbsp soy sauce, 1 tbsp honey, 1 minced garlic glove, 1/2 tsp ground cumin, salt &pepper. Thread the chicken onto skewers and grill or bake until cooked.

INGREDIENTS (1 SERVING)

- 1/2 cup (120 ml) cranberry juice
- 1/4 cup (60 ml) orange juice
- 1/2 cup (120 ml) sparkling water
- 1-2 teaspoons honey or agave syrup
- Ice cubes
- Orange slices or cranberries (for garnish)

STEPS

1. In a glass, combine cranberry juice, orange juice, sparkling water, and honey or agave syrup. Stir well to dissolve the sweetener.
2. Fill the glass with ice cubes.
3. Give it a gentle stir to combine the flavors.
4. Garnish with orange slices or cranberries (optional).
5. Serve chilled.

NUTRITIONAL FACTS & SERVING SUGGESTIONS

Cranberry Orange Salsa with Tortilla Chips: In a blender, pulse 1 cup of cranberries until finely chopped. In a bowl, combine the cranberries, 1 orange, peeled and segmented, 1/4 cup diced red onion, 1 diced jalapeño pepper, 1 tbsp chopped cilantro, 1 tbsp lime juice, 1tsp honey, and a pinch of salt. Stir well. Let the salsa sit in the refrigerator for at least 30 min to allow the flavors to meld together. Serve chilled with tortilla chips for dipping.

CRANBERRY SANGRIA

INGREDIENTS (4 SERVINGS)

- 1 cup ice cubes
- 1/4 pineapple, peeled, cut into wedges
- 1/2 small orange, thinly sliced, cut into wedges
- 1 passionfruit, quartered
- 2 cups (480 ml) cranberry juice
- 2 cups (480 ml) ginger beer
- 1/2 cup fresh mint leaves

NUTRITIONAL FACTS & SERVING SUGGESTIONS

Brie and Cranberry Crostini: Preheat the oven to 350°F (175°C). Place 4 slices of baguette on a baking sheet and toast them in the oven until lightly crispy. Remove from the oven and place a small slice of Brie cheese on each one. Return to the oven and bake until the cheese is melted. Let them cool for a minute or two. Top each crostini with approximately 1/2 tbsp of cranberry sauce or relish.

STEPS

1. Divide the ice cubes among 4 large serving glasses. Top with pineapple, orange, and passionfruit.
2. Divide the cranberry juice and ginger beer among the glasses.
3. Top with mint leaves.

CREAMY COCONUT BLACKBERRY MOJITO

INGREDIENTS (1 SERVING)

- 1/2 cup (120 g) blackberries
- 6-8 fresh mint leaves
- 2 tablespoons (30 ml) lime juice
- 2 tablespoons (30 ml) agave syrup, maple syrup, or honey (or adjust according to desired sweetness)
- 1/4 cup (60 ml) coconut cream
- 1/2 cup (120 ml) soda water
- Crushed ice
- Additional blackberries and mint leaves for garnish (optional)

STEPS

1. In a glass or cocktail shaker, muddle the blackberries and fresh mint leaves until well crushed and juicy.
2. Add lime juice and desired syrup to the muddled mixture and stir to combine.
3. Stir in the coconut cream until well incorporated.
4. Fill a glass with crushed ice.
5. Pour the blackberry mixture over the ice.
6. Top with soda water and gently stir.
7. Garnish with additional blackberries and mint leaves.

NUTRITIONAL FACTS & SERVING SUGGESTIONS

Blackberry Bruschetta: Toast slices of baguette and spread a layer of cream cheese. Top each slice with a spoonful of mashed blackberries and garnish with a fresh mint leaf. This appetizer balances the sweetness of the blackberries with the tanginess of the cheese, creating a delightful contrast of flavors.

- 1/2 cup cucumber juice (freshly juiced or store-bought)
- 1/4 cup freshly squeezed lime juice
- 1-2 teaspoons of honey or agave syrup
- 1 cup sparkling water or soda water
- Ice cubes
- Lemon slices and cucumber skewers for garnish (optional)

NUTRITIONAL FACTS & SERVING SUGGESTIONS

Cucumbers are hydrating fruits that provide vitamin K, vitamin C, and dietary fiber, promoting hydration and supporting immune function.

Greek Cucumber Bites: Slice cucumbers into rounds and top each one with a dollop of Greek yogurt. Sprinkle with chopped fresh dill and garnish with a lemon slice.

STEPS

1. In a glass, combine the cucumber juice, freshly squeezed lime juice, agave syrup or honey, and sparkling water. Stir well to dissolve the sweetener.
2. Fill the glass with ice cubes.
3. Give it a gentle stir to combine the flavors.
4. Garnish with lemon slices and cucumber skewers.
5. Serve chilled.

- 2 tablespoons (30 ml) elderflower syrup
- 3/4 cup (180 ml) sparkling water
- Squeeze fresh lemon juice
- Lemon twist for garnish (optional)

NUTRITIONAL FACTS &
SERVING SUGGESTIONS

Prosciutto-Wrapped Melon Skewers: Take a piece of melon and wrap it with a strip of prosciutto. Slide the prosciutto-wrapped melon onto a wooden skewer. Repeat the process until you have the desired number of skewers. Garnish each skewer with a fresh basil leaf.

STEPS

1. Fill a glass with ice cubes.
2. Pour the elderflower syrup over the ice.
3. Add the sparkling water and a squeeze of fresh lemon juice.
4. Stir gently to mix the flavors.
5. Garnish with a lemon twist, if desired.

- 2 cups (475 ml) frozen pineapple
- ½ cup (120 ml) frozen passionfruit
- 2 limes juiced
- ¼ cups (60 ml) ginger shot
- 1 cup (240 ml) cold water divided
- ¼ cups (60 ml) sparkling water

STEPS

1. Add all ingredients except sparkling water and plain water to a blender. Mix well, and add a dash of water as needed (just as much as is needed to get your blender to work well).
2. When everything is mixed together well, add the rest of the water and mix quickly.
3. Pour into glasses, top with sparking water, and serve.

NUTRITIONAL FACTS & SERVING SUGGESTIONS

Pineapple Salsa with Tortilla Chips: In a bowl, combine 2 cups diced pineapple, 1/2 cup red bell pepper, 1/4 cup red onion, 1 jalapeno pepper, and 2 tablespoons chopped cilantro. Squeeze the juice of 1 lime over the mixture and season with salt and pepper. Gently toss everything together until well combined. Taste and adjust the seasoning if needed. Allow the salsa to sit for about 15-20 minutes to let the flavors meld together. Serve with tortilla chips for dipping.

- 1 cup (240 ml) ginger ale
- 2 tablespoons (30 ml) fresh lemon juice
- Sparkling water (to top)
- Honey or agave syrup to taste
- Ice cubes

STEPS

1. In a glass, combine ginger ale and fresh lemon juice.
2. Add sparkling water to fill the glass.
3. Stir well.
4. Add agave syrup or honey to taste.
5. Serve chilled.

NUTRITIONAL FACTS & SERVING SUGGESTIONS

Zesty Chicken Skewers: In a bowl, combine 2 tbsp olive oil, 2 tbsp lemon juice, 1 tsp paprika, 1 tsp garlic powder, 1 tsp dried oregano, salt, and pepper. Add 1 pound (450 g) chicken breasts cut into cubes to the marinade and toss until evenly coated. Marinate for at least 30 minutes in the refrigerator. Preheat your grill or stovetop grill pan over medium-high heat. Thread the marinated chicken onto skewers. Grill the chicken skewers for about 8-10 minutes, turning occasionally, until the chicken is cooked through and slightly charred.

INGREDIENTS (1 SERVING)

- 10 - 12 leaves of fresh mint
- 2 tablespoons ginger ale soda syrup
- 1 teaspoon honey (optional)
- Freshly squeezed juice of 1 lime
- Sparkling water

STEPS

1. Gently muddle the mint leaves with the back of a wooden spoon.
2. Squeeze the juice of a lime and put it in a glass. Add the honey and stir, then add the mint leaves.
3. Add 2 tablespoons of ginger ale soda syrup.
4. Fill the glass with ice.
5. Top with sparkling water and stir to combine.
6. Garnish with lime and/or fresh mint.

NUTRITIONAL FACTS & SERVING SUGGESTIONS

Herbed Tomato Bruschetta: Preheat the oven to 375°F (190°C). Place 4 slices of baguette on a baking sheet and toast until they are golden and crisp. In a bowl, combine 2 diced ripe tomatoes, 2 tbsp of chopped fresh basil, 1 tbsp of chopped fresh parsley, 1 minced clove of garlic, 2 tbsp of olive oil, and season with salt and black pepper. Mix well. Remove the toasted bread slices and let them cool slightly. Spoon the herbed tomato mixture onto each bread slice, dividing it evenly.

GINGER PEACH FIZZ

INGREDIENTS (1 SERVING)

- 1 ripe peach, peeled and pitted
- 1-inch (2,5 cm) piece of fresh ginger, grated
- Juice of 1 lemon
- 1 cup (240ml) sparkling water
- Ice cubes

STEPS

1. In a blender, blend the ripe peach until smooth.
2. In a glass, muddle the grated ginger with the lemon juice.
3. Add the peach puree to the glass and stir well to combine.
4. Fill the glass with ice cubes and pour sparkling water over the ice.
5. Give it a gentle stir and garnish with a peach slice or a lemon wedge.

NUTRITIONAL FACTS & SERVING SUGGESTIONS

Peaches contain vitamin C, vitamin A, and dietary fiber, contributing to healthy skin, eye health, and digestion.

Greek Salad Skewers: Take skewers or toothpicks and thread 2 cherry tomatoes, followed by 2 cubes of cucumber, 2 Kalamata olives, and 2 cubes of feta cheese onto each one. In a small bowl, whisk together 2 tbsp of olive oil, 1 tbsp of lemon juice, 1 tsp of dried oregano, salt, and pepper. Drizzle the dressing over the skewers just before serving.

- ¼ cup (60 ml) maple syrup
- ¼ cup (60 ml) water
- ¼ cup (60 ml) thinly sliced ginger
- ¼ cup (60 ml) pumpkin purée
- ½ cup (120 ml) water
- 1 cup (240 ml) chilled sparkling water

NUTRITIONAL FACTS & SERVING SUGGESTIONS

Pumpkin is a rich source of vitamins A, C, and E. It also contains minerals such as potassium, magnesium, and iron.

Spiced Pumpkin Bites: Mix 1 cup of canned pumpkin purée with 1/4 tsp of cinnamon, 1/4 tsp of nutmeg, and a pinch of salt. Spread the mixture on toasted baguette slices and top with a dollop of whipped cream and a sprinkle of cinnamon.

STEPS

1. Add the maple syrup, 1/4 cup (60 ml) water, and ginger slices to a small saucepan. Heat over medium heat until it boils. Turn off the heat and let it rest for 1/2 hour.
2. Prepare the pumpkin juice by blending the pumpkin purée with 1/2 cup (120 ml) water.
3. Remove the ginger slices from the syrup and divide it between two glasses. Pour ¼ cup of the pumpkin juice into each glass and stir.
4. Pour ½ cup of cold sparkling water into each glass.

INGREDIENTS (1 SERVING)

- 1/2 cup (120 ml) unsweetened grapefruit juice
- 1/4 cup (60 ml) freshly squeezed lime juice
- 1-2 teaspoons of agave syrup or honey
- 1 cup sparkling water
- Ice cubes
- Grapefruit slices or a rosemary sprig, for garnish (optional)

NUTRITIONAL FACTS & SERVING SUGGESTIONS

Grapefruits are rich in vitamin C, provide dietary fiber, and contain antioxidants that contribute to healthy skin and immune support.

Citrus Avocado Bruschetta: Mash one ripe avocado and mix it with the juice of half a lime, a pinch of salt, and a dash of black pepper. Spread the avocado mixture on toasted baguette slices and top with grapefruit segments and a drizzle of honey.

STEPS

1. In a glass, combine the unsweetened grapefruit juice, freshly squeezed lime juice, honey or agave syrup, and sparkling water. Stir well to dissolve the sweetener.
2. Fill the glass with ice cubes.
3. Give it a gentle stir to combine the flavors.
4. Garnish with grapefruit slices or mint leaves.
5. Serve chilled.

GRAPEFRUIT GINGER MOCKTAIL

INGREDIENTS (2 SERVINGS)

- 1 cup (240 ml) pink grapefruit juice, chilled
- 1 cup (240 ml) ginger ale, chilled, sweetened with agave syrup
- 1 teaspoon ginger juice
- 2 slices fresh grapefruit or orange for garnish

STEPS

1. Add equal parts of grapefruit juice and ginger ale to a chilled glass.
2. Add ginger juice.
3. Garnish with a wedge of grapefruit or orange and serve.

NUTRITIONAL FACTS & SERVING SUGGESTIONS

Ginger Citrus Skewers: Skewer pieces of fresh grapefruit and orange alternately onto wooden skewers. In a small bowl, mix together 1 tablespoon of ginger juice, 1 tablespoon of honey or agave syrup, and a pinch of salt. Brush the ginger mixture onto the citrus skewers and grill them for a few minutes until slightly caramelized. These skewers provide a delightful balance of tangy citrus and warm ginger that pairs beautifully with the mocktail.

- 1 cup (40 g) spinach leaves
- 1/2 cup (120 ml) pineapple juice
- 1/2 cup (120 ml) apple juice
- 1/2 lime, juiced
- Ice cubes
- Pineapple slice or mint sprig, for garnish (optional)

NUTRITIONAL FACTS & SERVING SUGGESTIONS

Spinach is a good source of iron, calcium, and vitamins A and C.

Spinach and Feta Pinwheels: Roll out a sheet of puff pastry and spread a layer of crumbled feta cheese and chopped spinach leaves over it. Roll it tightly into a log and slice it into pinwheels. Bake the pinwheels in a preheated oven until golden and crispy. These pinwheels offer a savory and flaky texture that pairs well with the vibrant flavors of the mocktail.

STEPS

1. In a blender, combine the fresh spinach leaves, pineapple juice, apple juice, and lime juice.
2. Blend until you have a smooth and vibrant green mixture.
3. Fill a glass with ice cubes.
4. Pour the green mixture over the ice, filling the glass about halfway.
5. Stir gently to mix the flavors.
6. Garnish with a pineapple slice or mint sprig, if desired.

INGREDIENTS (2 SERVINGS)

- 2 cups (480 ml) brewed hibiscus tea (unsweetened)
- 1/4 cup (60 ml) freshly squeezed lemon juice
- 1-2 teaspoons of agave syrup or honey
- Ice cubes
- Lemon slices or fresh mint leaves for garnish (optional)

NUTRITIONAL FACTS & SERVING SUGGESTIONS

Hibiscus tea is rich in antioxidants and has been associated with reduced blood pressure and improved liver health.

Strawberry Bruschetta: Spread a layer of cream cheese on toasted baguette slices and top them with sliced strawberries. Drizzle a balsamic glaze or honey over the strawberries for added sweetness and flavor.

STEPS

1. In a pitcher, combine the brewed hibiscus tea, freshly squeezed lemon juice, and honey or agave syrup. Stir well to dissolve the sweetener.
2. Fill serving glasses with ice cubes.
3. Pour the hibiscus tea mixture over the ice.
4. Give it a gentle stir to combine the flavors.
5. Garnish with lemon slices or fresh mint leaves.
6. Serve chilled.

HIBISCUS SANGRIA

INGREDIENTS (6 SERVINGS)

- 6 hibiscus tea bags
- 3 cups (720 ml) almost-boiling water
- 3 cups (720 ml) cold water
- 1 apple, chopped
- 1 orange, with peel, sliced

STEPS

1. In a large container, steep the tea bags in hot water for 8 minutes. Discard the tea bags.
2. In a pitcher, combine the tea, cold water, and fruit. Refrigerate until the tea is chilled.
3. Serve over ice, add more chopped fruit if desired.

Variation: Try berry or peach tea and fruits like berries, plums, and peaches.

HONEYDEW REFRESHER

INGREDIENTS (2 SERVINGS)

- 1 cup (240 ml) fresh honeydew melon juice (freshly juiced or store-bought)
- 1/4 cup (60 ml) freshly squeezed lime juice
- 1 cup (240 ml) sparkling water
- Ice cubes
- Honeydew melon balls or mint leaves for garnish (optional)

NUTRITIONAL FACTS & SERVING SUGGESTIONS

Honeydew melon is a hydrating fruit that is low in calories and high in vitamin C. It also contains potassium.

Honeydew and Prosciutto Skewers: Cut honeydew melon into bite-sized cubes and wrap each cube with a slice of prosciutto. Thread the wrapped melon pieces onto skewers, alternating with fresh basil leaves. Drizzle the skewers with a balsamic glaze for an extra burst of flavor.

STEPS

1. In a pitcher, combine the melon juice, and freshly squeezed lime juice. Stir well.
2. Fill serving glasses with ice cubes. Pour the honeydew melon mixture over the ice.
3. Top each glass with sparkling water to add a refreshing fizz.
4. Give it a gentle stir to combine the flavors.
5. Garnish with honeydew melon balls or mint leaves. Serve chilled.

INGREDIENTS (4 SERVINGS)

- 1 cup tiger nuts
- 4 cups water
- 1 cinnamon stick
- 1/2 teaspoon vanilla extract
- Granulated sugar or agave syrup (adjust to taste)

Tiger nuts are rich in fiber and contain potassium and magnesium. They are a good source of healthy fats and are naturally gluten-free.

STEPS

1. Place the tiger nuts in a bowl and cover them with water. Let them soak for at least 8 hours.
2. Drain the soaked tiger nuts and transfer them to a blender. Add 2 cups of water and blend on high speed until you have a smooth and creamy mixture.
3. Place a fine-mesh strainer over a large bowl. Pour the mixture through the strainer, using a spoon or spatula to press down and extract as much liquid as possible.
4. Return the extracted liquid to the blender. Add the cinnamon stick, vanilla extract, and sugar.

5. Blend for an additional 1 to 2 minutes until well combined.
6. Remove the cinnamon stick from the blender and discard.
7. Taste and adjust the sweetness by adding more sugar if desired.
8. Chill in the refrigerator for at least 1 to 2 hours.
9. Stir well before serving.
10. Serve with chocolate chip cookies.

- 1/4 cup (60 ml) jasmine tea (brewed and cooled)
- 1/4 cup f(60 ml) freshly squeezed lemon juice
- 1-2 teaspoons agave syrup or honey
- 1 cup (240 ml) sparkling water
- Ice cubes
- Lemon slices or jasmine flowers for garnish

NUTRITIONAL FACTS & SERVING SUGGESTIONS

Lemon Herb Baked Chicken Wings: In a bowl, combine 1 pound of chicken wings with 1/4 cup of freshly squeezed lemon juice, 2 minced garlic cloves, 1 tablespoon of chopped fresh herbs (such as thyme and rosemary), 1 teaspoon of salt, and 1/2 teaspoon of black pepper. Let the wings marinate for at least 30 minutes. Then, bake them in a preheated oven at 425°F (220°C) for about 25-30 minutes until they are golden and crispy.

STEPS

1. In a glass, combine the jasmine tea, freshly squeezed lemon juice, and agave syrup or honey. Stir well to dissolve the sweetener.
2. Fill the glass with ice cubes.
3. Top with sparkling water to add a refreshing fizz.
4. Give it a gentle stir to combine the flavors.
5. Garnish with lemon slices or jasmine flowers.
6. Serve chilled.

INGREDIENTS (1 SERVING)

- 1 part passionfruit juice (or peach juice)
- 2 parts pineapple juice
- 2 parts orange juice
- 4 parts cranberry juice
- Ice cubes
- 1 orange slice for garnish (optional)

STEPS

1. Pour all juices into a shaker and add 1-2 ice cubes. Close the lid tightly and shake for 15 seconds.
2. Place ice cubes in a glass and pour over the mocktail. Decorate and serve.

NUTRITIONAL FACTS & SERVING SUGGESTIONS

Mini Ham and Cheese Sliders: Cut dinner rolls in half and layer thin slices of ham and your favorite cheese on the bottom half. Place the top half of the rolls over the fillings. Brush the tops with melted butter and sprinkle with poppy seeds or sesame seeds if desired. Bake in the oven at 350°F (175°C) for about 10-15 minutes or until the cheese is melted and the sliders are lightly toasted. These savory and satisfying sliders provide a delightful combination of flavors that pair perfectly with the fruity mocktail.

- 2 ripe kiwis, peeled and sliced
- Juice of 2 limes
- 6-8 fresh mint leaves
- 1 tablespoon honey or agave syrup
- 1 cup (240ml) sparkling water
- Ice cubes
- Kiwi slice for garnish (optional)

NUTRITIONAL FACTS & SERVING SUGGESTIONS

Kiwi is a nutrient-rich fruit that is high in vitamin C, vitamin K, and dietary fiber.

Kiwi Lime Salsa and Tortilla Chips: In a bowl, combine 2 ripe kiwis (peeled and sliced), the juice of 2 limes, 6-8 fresh mint leaves (finely chopped), and 1 tablespoon of honey or agave syrup. Mix well and let the flavors meld for a few minutes. Serve the kiwi lime salsa with crispy tortilla chips for a zesty and crunchy accompaniment to the mocktail.

STEPS

1. In a blender, puree the ripe kiwis until smooth.
2. In a glass, muddle the fresh mint leaves with lime juice and honey or agave syrup.
3. Add the kiwi puree to the glass and stir well to combine.
4. Fill the glass with ice cubes and pour sparkling water over the ice.
5. Give it a gentle stir and garnish with a kiwi slice.

INGREDIENTS (2 SERVINGS)

- 3/4 cup (180 ml) of carbonated ginger kombucha
- 1/4 cup (60 ml) oat creamer
- 2 tablespoons (30 ml) honey

STEPS

1. Add oat creamer and honey to a shaker with ice and shake until chilled.
2. Add kombucha to a glass with ice. Strain oat creamer and honey mixture over kombucha to create a frothy head.

NUTRITIONAL FACTS & SERVING SUGGESTIONS

Honey-Glazed Almonds: In a small saucepan, melt 2 tablespoons (30 grams) of butter over medium heat. Add 1 cup (120 grams) of raw almonds and cook for a few minutes, stirring frequently, until they start to turn golden. Drizzle in 2 tablespoons (30 ml) of honey and continue to cook for another minute until the almonds are coated and sticky. Spread the almonds on a parchment-lined baking sheet and let them cool completely. These crunchy and sweet honey-glazed almonds will provide a delightful contrast to the mocktail.

LAVENDER LEMONADE

- 2 tablespoons dried culinary lavender
- 1/4 cup (60 ml) freshly squeezed lemon juice
- 1-2 teaspoons honey or agave syrup
- 1 cup sparkling water
- Ice cubes
- Lemon slices or lavender sprigs for garnish (optional)

STEPS

1. In a small bowl, combine the lavender with 1/2 cup of hot water. Let it steep for about 10 minutes.
2. Strain the lavender-infused water, discard the lavender buds, and let it cool.
3. In a glass, combine the infused lavender water, lemon juice, and sweetener. Stir well.
4. Fill the glass with ice cubes. Top with sparkling water or soda water.
5. Stir gently and garnish.

NUTRITIONAL FACTS & SERVING SUGGESTIONS

Lemon Lavender Shortbread Cookies: In a mixing bowl, combine 1 cup (125 grams) of all-purpose flour, 1/4 cup (50 grams) of granulated sugar, 2 tablespoons of dried culinary lavender, and a pinch of salt. Add 1/2 cup (113 grams) of softened butter and mix until a dough forms. Roll the dough into a log, wrap it in plastic wrap, and refrigerate for about 30 minutes. Slice the chilled dough into cookies, place them on a baking sheet, and bake at 325°F (165°C) for 12-15 minutes or until the edges are golden.

- 1/4 cup (60 ml) lemon juice
- 1-2 tablespoons honey or agave syrup
- 1/4 cup (60 ml) water
- Ice
- Sugar, for rimming the glass
- Lemon or lime slice for garnish (optional)

Lemon Poppy Seed Bites: In a mixing bowl, combine 1 cup (120 grams) of almond flour, 1 tablespoon of lemon zest, 1 tablespoon of poppy seeds, 2 tablespoons of honey or agave syrup, and 1 tablespoon of melted coconut oil. Mix well until the mixture comes together. Roll the mixture into small bite-sized balls and refrigerate for about 30 minutes to firm up. These zesty and nutty Lemon Poppy Seed Bites provide a delightful and nutritious accompaniment to the mocktail.

1. In a shaker, combine the lemon juice, honey, water, and ice.
2. Shake until the ingredients are well mixed and the shaker is frosted.
3. Strain the mixture into a sugar-rimmed martini glass.
4. Garnish with a slice of lemon or lime.

INGREDIENTS (1 SERVING)

- 1 cup (240 ml) fresh mango juice
- 1/4 cup (60 ml) freshly squeezed lime juice
- 1-2 teaspoons honey or agave syrup
- 1 cup (240 ml) sparkling water
- Ice cubes
- Mango slices or mint leaves for garnish (optional)

NUTRITIONAL FACTS & SERVING SUGGESTIONS

Mangos are rich in vitamin C and vitamin A, and they also provide potassium and dietary fiber, benefiting immune health and eye health.

Mango Coconut Energy Balls: In a food processor, combine 1 cup of dried mango, 1 cup (80 grams) of unsweetened shredded coconut, 1/4 cup (30 grams) of raw cashews, 2 tablespoons of chia seeds, 2 tablespoons of honey or agave syrup, and a pinch of salt. Process until the mixture comes together and forms a sticky dough. Roll the mixture into small balls and refrigerate for about 30 minutes to firm up.

STEPS

1. In a pitcher, combine the fresh mango juice, freshly squeezed lime juice, and sweetener. Stir well to dissolve the sweetener.
2. Fill serving glasses with ice cubes.
3. Pour the mango mixture over the ice.
4. Top with sparkling water.
5. Give it a gentle stir to combine the flavors.
6. Garnish with mango slices or mint leaves.
7. Serve chilled.

INGREDIENTS (1 SERVING)

- 2 medium-sized ripe tomatoes
- 4-5 fresh basil leaves
- 1/2 lemon, juiced
- 1 tablespoon honey (optional, adjust to taste)
- Club soda or sparkling water
- Ice cubes
- Basil sprig or cherry tomato, for garnish (optional)

NUTRITIONAL FACTS & SERVING SUGGESTIONS

Tomato Bruschetta Cups: Preheat the oven to 375°F (190°C) and lightly grease a muffin tin. Cut circles of bread that fit into the muffin cups and press them gently into the tin to form cups. Brush the bread cups with olive oil and bake until golden and crisp. In a bowl, combine diced ripe tomatoes, chopped fresh basil, minced garlic, a drizzle of balsamic vinegar, and a pinch of salt and pepper. Spoon the tomato mixture into the bread cups and garnish with a basil leaf.

STEPS

1. Cut the tomatoes into chunks and remove the seeds.
2. In a blender, combine the tomato chunks, basil leaves, lemon juice, and honey if using.
3. Blend until you have a smooth mixture.
4. Fill a glass with ice cubes.
5. Pour the tomato and basil mixture over the ice, filling the glass about halfway.
6. Top up the glass with club soda or sparkling water.
7. Stir gently to mix the flavors.
8. Garnish with a basil sprig or cherry tomato, if desired.

MIMOSA MOCKTAIL

- 2 cups (480 ml) fresh orange juice (no pulp)
- 2 cups (480 ml) sparkling white grape juice or sparkling lemonade
- Fresh orange slices for garnish (optional)

NUTRITIONAL FACTS & SERVING SUGGESTIONS

Orange Creamsicle Dip: In a bowl, mix 1 cup (240 grams) of whipped cream cheese, 1/4 cup (60 grams) of powdered sugar, 1 teaspoon of vanilla extract, and 2 tablespoons (30 ml) of orange juice until smooth and creamy. Serve the dip with orange segments or graham crackers for a delightful and creamy treat.

STEPS

1. In a pitcher, gently mix together the orange juice and sparkling juice to combine.
2. Pour the mimosa evenly into 4 chilled glasses.
3. Add garnishes to the rim of each glass and serve chilled.

INGREDIENTS (1 SERVING)

- 1 lime cut into wedges
- 20 fresh mint leaves
- ⅔ cups (150 ml) of soda water or sparkling water
- Crushed ice

STEPS

1. Place the lime wedges and mint leaves in a highball glass, and squeeze in some of the juice from the lime wedges before adding them. Muddle together until most of the juice has been released from the lime.
2. Add in crushed ice, mix, and top with soda water. Decorate with a straw and a sprig of mint and serve immediately.

NUTRITIONAL FACTS & SERVING SUGGESTIONS

Mini Lime-Mint Tartle: Prepare mini tart shells by pressing a store-bought pie crust into a mini muffin tin and baking according to the package instructions. In a bowl, mix 1/2 cup (120 grams) of cream cheese, 2 tablespoons (30 grams) of powdered sugar, and 1 tablespoon (15 ml) of lime juice until smooth. Fill each tartlet with the lime-mint cream cheese mixture and garnish with a small mint leaf. These bite-sized tartlets will provide a delightful and tangy companion to the mocktail.

ORANGE CREAMSICLE

- 1 cup (240 ml) fresh orange juice
- 1/4 cup (60 ml) almond milk or coconut milk
- 1/2 teaspoon vanilla extract
- 1 tablespoon honey
- Ice cubes

STEPS

1. In a blender, combine fresh orange juice, almond milk, honey, and vanilla extract.
2. Blend until well combined and frothy.
3. Pour into a glass previously filled with ice.
4. Serve chilled.

NUTRITIONAL FACTS & SERVING SUGGESTIONS

Citrus Shrimp Skewers: Take around 12-16 medium-sized shrimp and marinate them in a mixture of 2 tablespoons of orange zest, 2 tablespoons of lemon juice, 2 cloves of minced garlic, and 2 tablespoons of olive oil. Skewer the shrimp and grill them for 2-3 minutes on each side until cooked through. Serve them with a tangy citrus dipping sauce made by combining 1/4 cup of orange juice, 2 tablespoons of lime juice, 2 tablespoons of honey, and a pinch of cayenne pepper.

- 1 cup (240 ml) orange juice
- 1 cup (240 ml) mango juice or puree
- 1/4 cup (60 ml) lime juice
- 2 tablespoons (30 ml) agave syrup
- 1 cup (240 ml) sparkling water
- Ice cubes
- Orange slices and mint leaves for garnish

NUTRITIONAL FACTS & SERVING SUGGESTIONS

Mango Avocado Salsa Cups: In a mixing bowl, combine 1 cup of diced mango, 1/2 cup of diced avocado, 1/4 cup of finely chopped red onion, 1/4 cup of chopped cilantro, and the finely chopped jalapeño. Squeeze the juice of 1 lime over the mixture and season with salt and pepper to taste. Gently toss all the ingredients together until well combined. Let the salsa sit for about 10 minutes to allow the flavors to meld together. Fill each small tortilla cup or bowl with the mango avocado salsa.

STEPS

1. In a pitcher, combine the fresh orange juice, mango juice, agave syrup, and lime juice. Stir well to mix all the ingredients together.
2. Add the sparkling water to the pitcher and gently stir to incorporate.
3. Fill glasses with ice cubes. Pour the mocktail mixture over the ice in each glass.
4. Garnish with orange slices and mint leaves, if desired.

- 1/2 cup (120 ml) orange juice
- 1 tablespoon (15 ml) lemon juice
- 1 tablespoon (15 ml) ginger syrup (store-bought or homemade)
- 1 cup (240 ml) sparkling water or ginger ale
- Ice cubes
- Orange zest or ginger slices for garnish (optional)

STEPS

1. In a glass, combine the freshly squeezed orange juice, lemon juice, and ginger syrup. Stir well to mix.
2. Fill the glass with ice cubes.
3. Pour the sparkling water or ginger ale over the ice and gently stir.
4. Garnish with orange zest or ginger slices, if desired.
5. Serve the orange ginger fizz mocktail immediately and enjoy!

NUTRITIONAL FACTS & SERVING SUGGESTIONS

Ginger Garlic Chicken Skewers: Cut boneless chicken breast into bite-sized pieces and marinate them in a mixture of 2 tablespoons of grated ginger, 2 cloves of minced garlic, 2 tablespoons of soy sauce, 1 tablespoon of honey, and a squeeze of lemon juice. Thread the chicken onto skewers and grill them until cooked through. Serve these flavorful skewers with a tangy ginger dipping sauce made by combining 1/4 cup of soy sauce, 1 tablespoon of grated ginger, 1 tablespoon of rice vinegar, and a teaspoon of honey.

ORANGE MOJITO MOCKTAIL

- 1/2 cup (120 ml) fresh orange juice
- 1/4 cup (60 ml) lime juice
- 8-10 fresh mint leaves
- 2 teaspoons agave syrup or honey
- 1 cup (240 ml) sparkling water
- Ice cubes
- Orange slices and additional mint leaves for garnish (optional)

STEPS

1. In a glass, muddle together the fresh mint leaves and agave syrup (or honey) to release the flavors.
2. Add the orange juice and lime juice to the glass. Stir well to combine.
3. Fill the glass with ice cubes.
4. Top the mixture with sparkling water and gently stir.
5. Garnish with orange slices and additional mint leaves, if desired.

NUTRITIONAL FACTS & SERVING SUGGESTIONS

Caprese Stuffed Tomatoes: Take tomatoes and hollow out the centers. Fill each tomato with a small mozzarella ball, a fresh basil leaf, and a sprinkle of chopped mint leaves. Drizzle the stuffed tomatoes with balsamic glaze for an elegant and flavorful appetizer.

INGREDIENTS (2 SERVINGS)

- Ripe papaya (5 to 6 big pieces)
- Pineapple (2 to 3 pieces)
- 1/2 cup (120 ml) orange juice
- 1/2 cup (120 ml) still or sparkling water

NUTRITIONAL FACTS & SERVING SUGGESTIONS

Papayas are packed with vitamin C, vitamin A, and digestive enzymes like papain, promoting immune function and digestion.

Teriyaki Chicken Skewers: In a bowl, combine 1/4 cup of soy sauce, 2 tbsp of honey, 1 tbsp of rice vinegar, minced garlic, grated ginger, sesame oil, salt, and pepper. Add 2 boneless, skinless chicken breasts, cut into bite-sized pieces, and toss to coat. Let marinate for at least 30 min. Thread the marinated chicken onto wooden skewers and grill until it is nicely charred. Serve alongside your choice of dipping sauce.

STEPS

1. Cut the fruits into big pieces.
2. Blend in a grinder and strain to remove any fruit fibers.
3. Add orange juice and still or sparkling water.
4. Serve chilled.

- 1/2 cup (120 ml) passionfruit juice
- 1 tablespoon lime juice
- Sparkling water (to top)
- Honey or agave syrup (to taste)

STEPS

1. In a glass, combine passion fruit juice and lime juice.
2. Add sparkling water to fill the glass.
3. Stir well.
4. Add honey or agave syrup to taste.
5. Serve chilled.

NUTRITIONAL FACTS & SERVING SUGGESTIONS

Passionfruit is a good source of vitamin C, providing around 50% of the daily recommended intake in half a cup of juice. It also contains dietary fiber, vitamin A, and potassium.

Tropical Bruschetta: Toast slices of baguette until crispy. Top them with a mixture of diced mango, pineapple, red bell pepper, red onion, cilantro, and a squeeze of lime juice. Sprinkle a hint of honey or agave syrup on top for a touch of sweetness.

PEACH BASIL MOCKTAIL

INGREDIENTS (4 SERVINGS)

- 4 ripe, skin-on, small to medium peaches
- Handful fresh basil
- 2 cups (480 ml) sparkling water

STEPS

1. Using a juicer, run the peaches through the juice extractor or place the peaches in a blender (for a smoothie texture).
2. Muddle the basil with the back of a wooden spoon (or chop it finely).
3. Divide peach juice and basil evenly among 4 flute glasses. Fill the glasses with sparkling water.
4. Serve chilled

NUTRITIONAL FACTS & SERVING SUGGESTIONS

Peaches are a good source of vitamin C and vitamin A, providing around 15% and 10% of the daily recommended intake, respectively, in a medium-sized peach with skin.

Basil Ricotta Crostini: Spread a layer of creamy ricotta cheese on toasted baguette slices. Top it with sliced ripe peaches and garnish with fresh basil leaves. Drizzle with a balsamic glaze for added tanginess.

- 1 cup (240 ml) peach nectar or peach juice
- 1/2 cup (120 ml) raspberry puree or raspberry juice
- 1/2 cup (120 ml) soda water
- 2 tablespoons (30 ml) grenadine syrup
- Crushed ice, to serve
- Fresh raspberries and mint sprigs for garnish (optional)

NUTRITIONAL FACTS & SERVING SUGGESTIONS

Baked Brie with Raspberry Jam: Place a wheel of Brie cheese on a baking dish and bake it until it becomes soft and gooey. Serve it with a dollop of raspberry jam or spread the jam on crackers or bread slices before topping them with the warm melted Brie. This combination of sweet and savory flavors pairs well with the mocktail.

STEPS

1. In a shaker or mixing glass, combine the peach nectar or peach juice with the raspberry juice.
2. Add the soda water and grenadine syrup to the mixture. Stir gently to combine all the ingredients.
3. Fill serving glasses with crushed ice.
4. Pour the mixture over the ice, dividing it evenly between the glasses.
5. Garnish with a sprig of mint.

INGREDIENTS (2-3 SERVINGS)

- 2 ripe peaches
- 1 large carrot
- 1 cup (240 ml) orange juice
- 1 tablespoon (15 ml) lemon juice
- Ice cubes

STEPS

1. Peel and pit the peaches. Chop them into small pieces.
2. Peel the carrot and cut it into small chunks.
3. In a blender, combine the chopped peaches, carrot chunks, orange juice, and lemon juice.
4. Blend on high speed until the mixture becomes smooth and well combined.
5. Fill serving glasses with ice cubes. Pour the Peach Carrot mixture over the ice, dividing it evenly between the glasses.

NUTRITIONAL FACTS & SERVING SUGGESTIONS

Carrot Fritters with Peach Salsa: Grate 1 large carrot and combine it with 1/2 cup of flour, 1 beaten egg, 1/4 cup of chopped onions, and a pinch of spices like cumin, paprika, and salt. Form the mixture into small patties and pan-fry them in a lightly oiled skillet until golden brown. Serve the carrot fritters with a tangy peach salsa made by combining 2 diced peaches, 1/4 cup of finely chopped red onion, 1/2 jalapeño (seeded and finely chopped for milder heat), the juice of 1 lime, and a handful of chopped cilantro.

- 4 tablespoons pear juice
- 1 tablespoon ginger syrup
- Sparkling water

For the ginger syrup:

- 1/2 cup (120 ml) sugar or substitute
- 1/2 cup (120 ml) water
- 1/2 cup (120 g) fresh ginger root, peeled and cut into small pieces

STEPS

1. Fill the glass with ice.
2. Add in pear juice, and ginger syrup, and top off with sparkling water.
3. Garnish with pear slice and sprig of rosemary (optional)

For the ginger syrup:

1. Combine sugar, water, and ginger in a small saucepan over medium heat and boil, stirring until sugar is dissolved. Simmer for 10 minutes.
2. Remove from heat and let sit for 20 minutes. Strain out ginger and let cool.

NUTRITIONAL FACTS & SERVING SUGGESTIONS

Pears are a good source of dietary fiber, vitamin C, and potassium, promoting digestive health and supporting immune function.

Ginger Soy Edamame: Boil 1 cup of fresh or frozen edamame. Drain them and toss them with a mixture of 1 tablespoon of ginger syrup, 1 tablespoon of soy sauce, and a sprinkle of sesame seeds.

- 1 cup (240ml) fresh pineapple juice
- 1-inch (2.5cm) piece of fresh ginger, grated
- 1 tablespoon fresh lime juice
- 1 cup (240ml) sparkling water
- Ice cubes

STEPS

1. In a shaker or glass, combine the fresh pineapple juice, grated ginger, and lime juice.
2. Shake or stir well to infuse the flavors.
3. Fill a glass with ice cubes and pour the mixture over the ice.
4. Top it off with sparkling water and give it a gentle stir.
5. Garnish with a slice of fresh pineapple or a lime wedge, if desired.

NUTRITIONAL FACTS & SERVING SUGGESTIONS

Pineapples contain vitamin C and manganese, as well as bromelain, an enzyme that aids digestion.

Ginger Glazed Shrimp Skewers: Thread 1 pound of peeled shrimp onto skewers. In a bowl, mix 1 tbsp of grated ginger, 2 tbsp of soy sauce, 1 tbsp of honey, and a splash of lime juice. Brush the mixture onto the shrimp and grill or broil until cooked through. Serve with a side of grilled pineapple wedges for a tasty pairing.

PIÑA COLADA MOCKTAIL

INGREDIENTS (2 SERVINGS)

- 2 cups (480 ml) fresh pineapple chunks
- 1 cup (240 ml) coconut milk
- 1/2 cup (120 ml) pineapple juice (unsweetened), or more coconut milk
- 2 tablespoons lime juice
- Pineapple wedges for garnish (optional)

STEPS

1. If using canned pineapple, drain and thoroughly rinse the pineapple chunks. If you want to cut your own fresh pineapple, cut it into bite-sized pieces.
2. Give the coconut milk a good shake. Then put it in the fridge for 15 minutes.
3. Add all of the ingredients to a high-speed blender. Blend until smooth.
4. Serve over some ice cubes and garnish with a pineapple wedge (optional)

NUTRITIONAL FACTS & SERVING SUGGESTIONS

Pineapple Avocado Salsa: Dice 1 cup (240g) of fresh pineapple and 1 ripe avocado. Combine them with 2 tablespoons of finely chopped red onion, 1/2 jalapeño (seeds removed for milder heat and finely chopped), a handful of chopped cilantro, the juice of 1 lime, and a pinch of salt. Toss everything together and serve this refreshing and tangy salsa with tortilla chips or cucumber slices for a lighter option.

POMEGRANATE MOCKTAIL WITH ORANGE

INGREDIENTS (4 SERVINGS)

- 1 1/2 cups (360 ml) pomegranate juice
- 1/2 cup (120 ml) freshly-squeezed orange juice
- 1 cup (240 ml) sparkling water
- 1 lime, sliced for garnish (optional)
- Crushed ice or ice cubes

STEPS

1. Divide the crushed ice between four cocktail glasses.
2. In a large pitcher, combine the pomegranate juice, and orange juice in a pitcher. Stir gently to combine.
3. Pour the mixture into your cocktail glasses and top with sparkling water.
4. Garnish with a slice of fresh lime, if desired.

NUTRITIONAL FACTS & SERVING SUGGESTIONS

Pomegranates are rich in antioxidants, vitamin C, and vitamin K, promoting heart health and providing immune support.

Citrus Avocado Salad: In a bowl, combine segments of 2 oranges and 2 grapefruits with 2 avocados (sliced). Add 4 cups of mixed greens, 1/4 cup of sliced red onion, and a sprinkle of 1/4 cup (35g) of toasted almonds. Drizzle with a citrus vinaigrette made from the juice of 1 orange, 1/2 lemon, 2 tbsp of olive oil, and 1 tbsp of honey. Toss everything together.

INGREDIENTS (1 SERVING)

- ¼ (60ml) cup pomegranate juice
- Juice of 1 lime
- 8-10 fresh mint leaves
- 1 tablespoon honey or sweetener of choice
- 1 cup (240ml) sparkling water
- Ice cubes

STEPS

1. In a glass, muddle the fresh mint leaves with the lime juice and honey.
2. Add pomegranate juice to the glass and stir well to combine.
3. Fill the glass with ice cubes and pour sparkling water over the ice.
4. Stir gently and garnish with a mint sprig.

NUTRITIONAL FACTS & SERVING SUGGESTIONS

Pomegranate Guacamole: Mash 1 ripe avocado with the juice of half a lime, 1 tablespoon of diced red onion, 1 teaspoon of minced garlic, 1 tablespoon of chopped cilantro, and a pinch of salt. Fold in 2 tablespoons of pomegranate arils for a burst of sweetness and added texture. Serve the pomegranate guacamole with crispy tortilla chips or vegetable sticks.

RASPBERRY LEMON MOCKTAIL

INGREDIENTS (1 SERVING)

- 1 cup (150 g) fresh or frozen raspberries
- 1 tablespoon fresh lemon juice
- 1 cup (240ml) sparkling water
- 1 teaspoon honey or sweetener of choice
- Ice cubes

STEPS

1. In a blender, puree the fresh raspberries until smooth.
2. Strain the raspberry puree through a fine-mesh sieve to remove the seeds.
3. In a glass, combine the raspberry puree, fresh lemon juice, sparkling water, and honey.
4. Stir well until the honey is dissolved.
5. Add ice cubes to the glass and serve chilled.

NUTRITIONAL FACTS & SERVING SUGGESTIONS

Raspberries are high in vitamin C and dietary fiber, and they contain antioxidants that promote healthy aging and heart health.

Goat Cheese and Raspberry Salad: In a bowl, combine 2 cups of mixed greens with 1 ounce of crumbled goat cheese, 1 tbsp of toasted walnuts, and a handful of fresh raspberries. In a separate small bowl, whisk together 1 tbsp of olive oil, 1 tsp of balsamic vinegar, a touch of Dijon mustard, and a pinch of salt & pepper. Drizzle the dressing over the salad and toss gently.

- 1/2 cup (120 ml) raspberry juice
- 4-6 fresh basil leaves
- 1 tablespoon lime juice
- 1 tablespoon agave syrup or honey
- 1/2 cup (120 ml) still or sparkling water
- Ice cubes
- Fresh raspberries and a sprig of rosemary for garnish (optional)

NUTRITIONAL FACTS & SERVING SUGGESTIONS

Spinach and Raspberry Salad: In a bowl, combine 2 cups (60g) of fresh spinach leaves with a handful of fresh raspberries, 1 tablespoon of sliced almonds, and 1 tablespoon of thinly sliced red onion. In a separate small bowl, whisk together 1 tablespoon of olive oil, 1 tablespoon of lime juice, 1 teaspoon of agave syrup (or honey), and a pinch of salt and pepper. Drizzle the dressing over the salad and toss gently to coat.

STEPS

1. In a glass, muddle together the fresh basil leaves and agave syrup (or honey) to release the flavors.
2. Add the raspberry juice and lime juice to the glass. Stir well to combine.
3. Fill the glass with ice cubes.
4. Top the mixture with still or sparkling water and gently stir.
5. Garnish with fresh raspberries and rosemary, if desired.

INGREDIENTS (1 SERVING)

- 1 tablespoon (15 ml) rose water
- 1/4 cup (60 ml) lemon juice
- 1/4 cup (60 ml) grenadine
- Baby rose or rose petals for garnish (optional)

STEPS

1. Add rose water, lemon juice, and grenadine to a tall glass with ice and gently stir to combine.

NUTRITIONAL FACTS & SERVING SUGGESTIONS

Cucumber and Cream Cheese Tea Sandwiches: Spread a thin layer of cream cheese on 2 slices of bread. Slice 1/4 cup (60g) of cucumber into thin rounds and arrange them evenly on one slice of bread. Sprinkle a pinch of salt over the cucumbers. Place the other slice of bread on top to form a sandwich. Cut off the crusts if desired, then cut the sandwich into small squares or triangles for bite-sized tea sandwiches.

- 1/2 cup (120ml) ginger ale
- 2 tablespoons (30ml) grenadine syrup
- Maraschino cherry for garnish (optional)
- Ice cubes

NUTRITIONAL FACTS & SERVING SUGGESTIONS

Cheese and Crackers Platter: Create a platter with an assortment of cheese slices or cubes, accompanied by an assortment of crackers. Choose a variety of cheeses like cheddar, gouda, brie, and blue cheese to provide different flavors and textures. Add some fresh grapes or sliced apples for a touch of freshness and color.

STEPS

1. Fill a glass with ice cubes.
2. Pour the ginger ale over the ice.
3. Add the grenadine syrup and stir gently to mix.
4. Garnish with a maraschino cherry.

INGREDIENTS (2-3 SERVINGS)

- 1/2 cup (125 gr) sliced strawberries
- 1/2 cup (125 gr) diced pineapple
- 1/2 cup (125 gr) sliced oranges
- 1/2 cup (125 gr) sliced kiwi
- 1/2 cup (125 gr) blueberries
- 1 cup (250 ml) sparkling water
- Ice cubes
- Fresh fruit slices for garnish (optional)

STEPS

1. In a pitcher, combine the fruit juice and sparkling water.
2. Stir well to mix.
3. Place a few ice cubes in each flute glass.
4. Pour the sparkling fruit punch over the ice cubes.
5. Garnish with fresh fruit slices (optional)
6. Serve immediately.

NUTRITIONAL FACTS & SERVING SUGGESTIONS

Spinach and Feta Phyllo Cups: Preheat the oven to 375°F (190°C). Take 12 pre-made phyllo pastry cups. In a bowl, combine 1 cup of chopped spinach and 1/2 cup of crumbled feta cheese. Spoon the spinach and feta mixture into the phyllo cups, distributing it evenly. Place the filled cups on a baking sheet and bake until the phyllo cups are golden brown and crispy. Let them cool slightly before serving.

INGREDIENTS (1 SERVING)

- 1/2 cup (120 ml) grape juice
- 2 tablespoons (30 ml) lemon juice
- 1/4 cup (60 ml) sparkling water
- Fresh grapes, for garnish

NUTRITIONAL FACTS & SERVING SUGGESTIONS

Grapes contain antioxidants, vitamin C, and dietary fiber, benefiting heart health and immune function.

Spinach and Artichoke Dip Stuffed Mushrooms: Remove the stems from 3-4 button mushrooms. In a bowl, combine 2 tbsp of cream cheese, 1 tbsp of chopped spinach, 1 tbsp of chopped artichoke hearts, 1 tbsp of grated Parmesan cheese, and a pinch of garlic powder. Mix well. Spoon the mixture into the mushroom caps. Sprinkle some additional Parmesan cheese on top. Bake at 375°F (190°C) until the filling is golden brown.

STEPS

1. Fill a glass with ice.
2. Add the grape juice and lemon juice to the glass.
3. Stir well to combine.
4. Top with sparkling water.
5. Garnish with fresh grapes.
6. Serve and enjoy!

SPARKLING PEAR MOCKTAIL

INGREDIENTS (2 SERVINGS)

- ¼ cup (7 g) fresh basil leaves
- ¼ cup (7 g) fresh mint
- ½ cup (120 ml) pear juice (no added sugar)
- 2 cups (480 ml) sparkling water

STEPS

1. Combine the pear juice in a small cup with 3 tablespoons of fresh mint and 3 tablespoons of basil. Muddle with the back of a wooden spoon.
2. Strain the juice into two separate glasses and top with ice.
3. Fill with sparkling water till full and garnish with basil and mint leaves.

NUTRITIONAL FACTS & SERVING SUGGESTIONS

Cucumber Avocado Bites: Slice 1 medium cucumber into thick rounds. In a bowl, mash ½ ripe avocado and mix it with 1 tablespoon of lemon juice, 1 tablespoon of finely chopped fresh basil, and 1 tablespoon of finely chopped fresh mint. Spread a small dollop of the avocado mixture onto each cucumber round. Optional: top each bite with a cherry tomato half or a sprinkle of black sesame seeds.

INGREDIENTS (2-3 SERVINGS)

- 1/4 pound (125 g) of fresh strawberries, washed, hulled
- 3/4 cup (180 ml) diet lemonade, chilled
- 1/2 cup (120 ml) unsweetened apple juice, chilled
- 1/2 cup (120 ml) sparkling water, chilled
- 1/4 cup (60 ml) freshly brewed tea, cooled
- A small handful of mint leaves
- Ice cubes, to serve

STEPS

1. In a blender, blend the strawberries until smooth.
2. In a pitcher or serving jug, combine the blended strawberries, lemonade, apple juice, sparkling water, and cooled tea. Stir well.
3. Add a small handful of mint leaves and gently stir again.
4. Fill serving glasses with ice cubes.
5. Pour the Strawberry Apple Punch into the glasses, dividing it evenly between the servings.

NUTRITIONAL FACTS & SERVING SUGGESTIONS

Strawberries are rich in vitamin C and antioxidants, supporting immunity and promoting healthy skin. They are low in calories and high in fiber.

Fresh Berries with Yogurt Dip: Take 1 cup of mixed fresh berries. Arrange them on a plate. For the yogurt dip, mix together 1/2 cup of Greek yogurt with a touch of honey and a sprinkle of finely chopped mint leaves. Serve the berries alongside the dip.

STRAWBERRY KIWI PUNCH

INGREDIENTS (2-3 SERVINGS)

- 1 cup strawberries, hulled and sliced
- 2 kiwis, peeled and sliced
- 1 tablespoon honey or agave syrup
- 1 cup (240 ml) sparkling water
- 1/2 cup (120 ml)apple juice
- Ice cubes
- Mint leaves for garnish (optional)

NUTRITIONAL FACTS & SERVING SUGGESTIONS

Greek Salad Skewers: Cut 6 cherry tomatoes in half. Cut 1/2 cucumber into bite-sized chunks. Cut 1/4 red onion into small wedges. Cut 1/4 cup of feta cheese into small cubes. Thread a cherry tomato half, a cucumber chunk, a red onion wedge, and a feta cheese cube onto each skewer. Optional: drizzle the skewers with a Greek dressing for extra flavor.

STEPS

1. In a blender, add the sliced strawberries, sliced kiwis, and honey or syrup. Blend until smooth.
2. Strain the strawberry and kiwi mixture through a fine-mesh sieve to remove any seeds or pulp.
3. In a pitcher, combine the strained mixture, sparkling water, and apple juice. Stir well.
4. Fill glasses with ice cubes and pour the punch over the ice. Garnish with mint.

SUNSET ZEN MOCKTAIL

- 1 large carrot, peeled and chopped
- 1-inch (1,25 cm) piece of fresh ginger, peeled and grated
- 1/2 lemon, juiced
- 1 tablespoon honey (adjust to taste)
- Sparkling water or ginger ale
- Ice cubes
- Carrot stick or fresh mint sprig, for garnish (optional)

STEPS

1. In a blender, combine the chopped carrot, grated ginger, lemon juice, and honey.
2. Blend until you have a smooth puree.
3. Fill a glass with ice cubes.
4. Pour the carrot and ginger mixture over the ice, filling the glass about halfway.
5. Top up the glass with sparkling water or ginger ale.
6. Stir gently to mix the flavors.
7. Garnish with a carrot stick or fresh mint sprig, if desired.

NUTRITIONAL FACTS & SERVING SUGGESTIONS

Spicy Roasted Chickpeas: Take 1/2 cup of cooked chickpeas and pat them dry. In a small bowl, mix together 1/2 tsp of olive oil, 1/4 tsp of ground cumin, 1/4 tsp of paprika, a pinch of cayenne pepper, and a sprinkle of salt. Toss the chickpeas in the spice mixture until coated evenly. Spread the chickpeas on a baking sheet and roast in a preheated oven at 400°F (200°C) until crispy.

INGREDIENTS (6 SERVINGS)

- 2 cups (480 ml) pineapple juice
- 1 1/2 (360 ml) cups apricot juice (or peach juice)
- 1 cup (240 ml) ginger beer
- 1 cup (240 ml) soda water
- 1/4 cup (60 ml) lime juice
- Crushed ice, to serve

STEPS

1. Place the pineapple juice, apricot juice, ginger beer, soda water, and lime juice in a large mixing jug and stir to combine.
2. Pour into a serving jug and add the ice.
3. Serve immediately.

NUTRITIONAL FACTS & SERVING SUGGESTIONS

Baked Apricot Brie Bites: Take 6 puff pastry squares and press them into mini muffin tins. Cut 6 small cubes of Brie cheese and place one cube into each pastry square. Top each Brie cube with a dollop of apricot jam. Bake in a preheated oven at 400°F (200°C) until the pastry is golden and the cheese is melted. Allow the bites to cool slightly before serving. These warm and cheesy apricot Brie bites provide a delightful combination of sweet and savory flavors.

VIRGIN MARGARITA

- 1/4 cup (60 ml) freshly squeezed lime juice
- 2 tablespoons freshly squeezed lemon juice
- 2 tablespoons freshly squeezed orange juice
- 1 tablespoon agave or maple syrup
- 1/4 to 1/2 cup (60-120 ml) seltzer/club soda/tonic water/sparkling water, to taste
- Flaky sea salt, for rimming
- Lime wedge, for rim and garnish (optional)

NUTRITIONAL FACTS & SERVING SUGGESTIONS

Zucchini Fritters: Grate 1 small zucchini and squeeze out any excess moisture. In a bowl, combine the grated zucchini with 1 beaten egg, 2 tablespoons of flour, 1 tablespoon of finely chopped green onion, 1 tablespoon of grated Parmesan cheese, and a pinch of salt and pepper. Heat a small amount of oil in a pan over medium heat. Drop spoonfuls of the zucchini mixture into the pan and flatten them slightly with the back of a spoon. Cook until golden brown on both sides.

STEPS

1. Rim a glass with salt (optional): Run a lime wedge around the rim of the glass and dip it in salt to create a salt rim.
2. Fill the glass with ice cubes and add the lime, lemon, and orange juices along with the agave or maple syrup. Stir well. The margarita is also excellent if you use a shaker.
3. Top the margarita with seltzer or club soda.
4. Garnish with a lime wedge.

INGREDIENTS (1 SERVING)

- 2 tablespoons (30 ml) lime juice
- 1 ½ tablespoons tomato paste
- 1 1/4 cups (300 ml) of citrus or ginger kombucha (any of your favorites will work as well)
- 2-3 dashes of hot sauce (optional)
- Lime wedge and salt for rim (optional)
- Lime wheel and cherry tomato to garnish (optional)

STEPS

1. Run a lime wedge along the rim of your glass, then dip the glass in salt (only on the outside of the rim).
2. Add lime juice, tomato paste, and hot sauce to the glass, and stir until smooth.
3. Gently pour in kombucha.
4. Give the mixture a stir to combine the ingredients, but gently enough that you don't remove the fizz from the kombucha.
5. Add ice, then garnish with a lime wheel and cherry tomato.

NUTRITIONAL FACTS & SERVING SUGGESTIONS

Spicy Tomato Bruschetta: In a small bowl, mix together 1 ½ tablespoons of tomato paste, 1 tablespoon of lime juice, and 2-3 dashes of hot sauce (optional). Toast a few slices of baguette or bread until lightly crisp. Spread the tomato mixture onto each toasted slice. Optional: sprinkle with grated Parmesan cheese and broil for a minute to melt the cheese. Garnish with a lime wheel and cherry tomato for an attractive presentation.

WATERMELON REFRESHER

- 3 cups (450 g) cubed watermelon (seedless)
- ¼ cup lime juice (2 limes). Slice 4 thin rounds and set aside for garnish.
- 2 cups (480 ml) club soda
- 8 sprigs of mint

STEPS

1. Cube watermelon. Remove any seeds.
2. Juice the limes and blend with the watermelon until smooth.
3. Using a sieve, strain the watermelon and lime mixture until you're left with just the juice. Set aside.
4. Place 5 mint leaves at the bottom of each glass. Fill with ice. Pour watermelon juice halfway full. Top with club soda until full. Gently stir.
5. Garnish each glass with a thin slice of watermelon, a sprig of mint, and a lime wedge.

NUTRITIONAL FACTS & SERVING SUGGESTIONS

Tabbouleh: Place 1 cup couscous in a bowl and pour 2 cups of warm water over it. Make sure the water covers the couscous. Let it sit until it has absorbed the water and expanded in size. Fluff the couscous with a fork to separate the grains. Combine the couscous, 1/2 cup mint leaves, 1 cup diced tomatoes, 1/2 cup diced cucumber, and 4 sliced green onions. In a small bowl, whisk together 2 tbsp of lemon juice, 4 tbsp of olive oil, salt, and pepper. Pour dressing over the couscous and toss well. Let the tabbouleh sit for 15-20 min to allow the flavors to meld together.

- 1/4 cup (60 ml) watermelon juice
- 2 tablespoons (30 ml) mixed berry juice (such as strawberry, raspberry, or blueberry)
- 1/4 cup (60 ml) sparkling water
- Watermelon slice, for garnish
- Fresh berries, for garnish

STEPS

1. Fill a glass with ice.
2. Add the watermelon juice and mixed berry juice to the glass.
3. Stir well to mix.
4. Top with sparkling water.
5. Garnish with a watermelon slice and fresh berries.
6. Serve and enjoy!

NUTRITIONAL FACTS & SERVING SUGGESTIONS

Caprese Stuffed Avocado Halves: Cut 1 ripe avocado in half and remove the pit. Scoop out a small portion of the flesh from each half to create a hollow cavity. In a small bowl, mix together 2-3 cherry tomatoes (quartered), 2-3 small fresh mozzarella balls (cut into small pieces), and a sprinkle of chopped fresh basil. Fill each avocado half with the Caprese mixture. Optional: drizzle with a balsamic reduction or a sprinkle of sea salt.

Made in United States
Troutdale, OR
04/05/2024

18858022R00053